A Visit to
CAMBODIA

Rob Alcraft

Heinemann
LIBRARY

First published in Great Britain by Heinemann Library,
Halley Court, Jordan Hill, Oxford OX2 8EJ,
a division of Reed Educational and Professional Publishing Ltd.

Heinemann is a registered trademark of Reed Educational & Professional Publishing Limited.

OXFORD MELBOURNE AUCKLAND
JOHANNESBURG BLANTYRE GABORONE
IBADAN PORTSMOUTH (NH) USA CHICAGO

Designed by AMR
Illustrations by Art Construction
Printed and bound in Hong Kong/China by South China Printing Co.

03 02 01 00 99
10 9 8 7 6 5 4 3 2 1

ISBN 0 431 08330 4

British Library Cataloguing in Publication Data

Alcraft, Rob, 1966–
   A visit to Cambodia. – (Heinemann first library)
   1.Cambodia – Juvenile literature
   I.Title II.Cambodia
   959.6

J 137.716
€ 10.15

Acknowledgements
The Publishers would like to thank the following for permission to reproduce photographs:
Colourific!: Michael Yamashita pp 13, 27, Catherine Karnow p 16; Hutchison Library: Sarah Murray p 10, Nigel Sitwell pp 14, 28; Link: Sue Carpenter p 24, Jan Knapik p 26; Network: Roger Hutchings p 19; Panos Pictures: Nic Dunlop pp 5, 21, Guiseppe Bizzarri p 7, Jim Holmes pp 8, 18, 22, Jon Spaull p 20, Irene Slegt p 23; Robert Harding Picture Library: Gavin Hellier p 25; Still Pictures: Gilles Martin p 6; Telegraph Colour Library: Masterfile p 29; Trip: A Gasson pp 9, 17, B. A. Dixie Dean p 11, Ask Images p 12, F Nichols p 15.

Cover photograph reproduced with permission of Robert Harding Picture Library.

Every effort has been made to contact copyright holders of any material reproduced in this book. Any omissions will be rectified in subsequent printings if notice is given to the Publisher.

Any words appearing in bold, **like this**, are explained in the Glossary.

Contents

Cambodia

ASIA

.:.Angkor Wat

Tonlé Sap Lake

Tonlé Sap River

Phnom Penh

North

GULF OF THAILAND

SOUTH CHINA SEA

Key
Land above 0m/sea level
Land over 500m
Land over 1000m
● Capital

This is a map of Cambodia. Cambodia is in Asia.

It is always warm in Cambodia.
The land is quite flat and very green.

Land

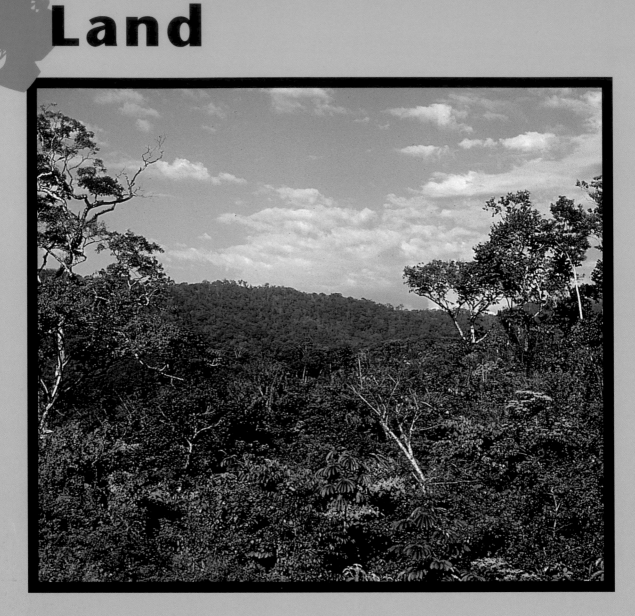

Cambodia has thick forests. Tall trees can grow 50 metres high. There are elephants, leopards and bears.

In Cambodia, winds called the **monsoons** bring heavy rain. For four or five months it pours with rain every day. The rain makes the **crops** grow.

Landmarks

Angkor Wat is a 900 year old **temple**. It is built from blocks of stone that fit perfectly together. It was once part of a great city.

There is a huge lake in the middle of
Cambodia, called the Tonlé Sap lake.
It is wide and shallow, and full of fish.

Homes

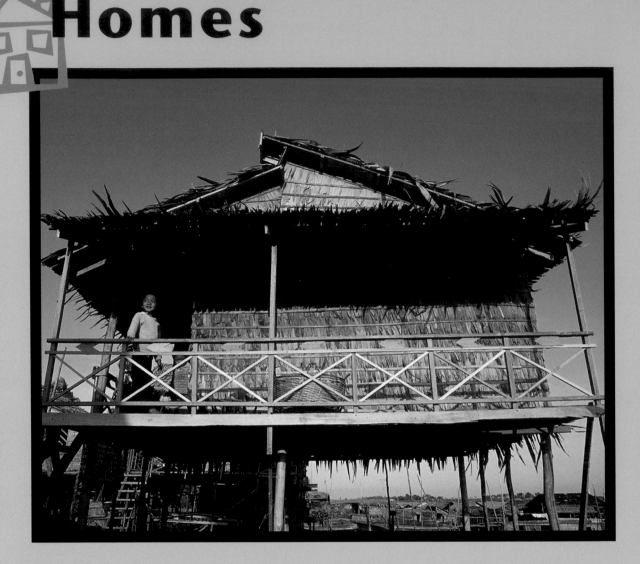

Most people in Cambodia live in the countryside. They build their homes up on **stilts**, to keep them dry and cool. They make roofs from **palm tree** leaves.

There is one big city in Cambodia. It is the **capital** city, called Phnom Penh. Here families live in small flats and houses, with one or two rooms.

Food

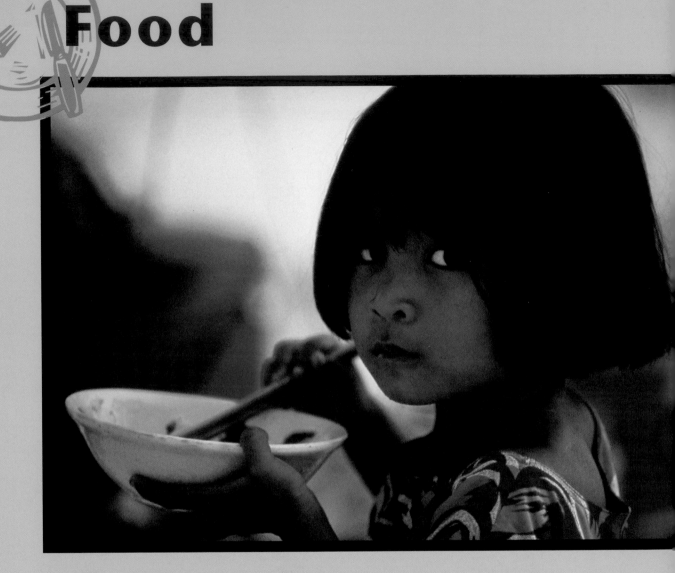

Cambodians eat with **chopsticks**. They eat lots of rice. Sometimes they add a sauce made of peanuts and fish, or a salad with herbs like garlic and mint.

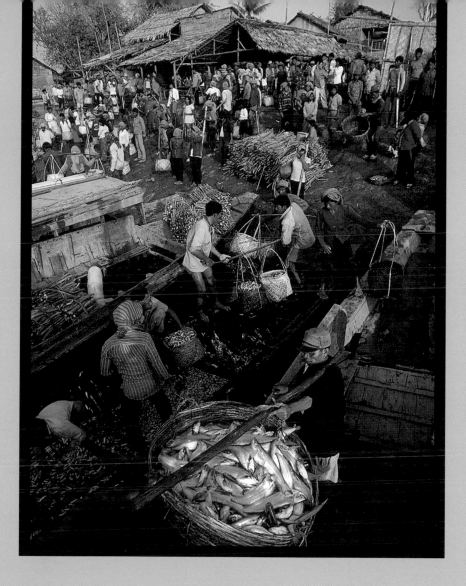

Fish is a favourite Cambodian food.
The fish is grilled and wrapped in
little parcels of lettuce leaves and
dipped in a spicy sauce.

Clothes

Cambodian clothes are light and cool.
Men and women wear a cloth that they
wrap around them like a skirt, or they
wear trousers. On top they wear a shirt.

Some young Cambodian men become
Buddhist monks. They wear bright orange
robes and shave their heads. They must
keep 227 difficult promises to be a monk.

Work

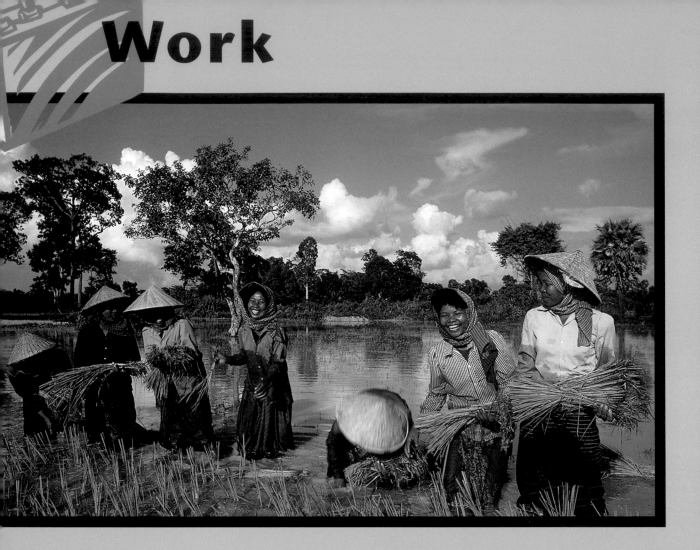

When the **monsoon** rains come, farmers
use **buffalo** to **plough** their fields.
Then they plant their fields with rice.
Each rice plant is pushed into the
muddy fields by hand.

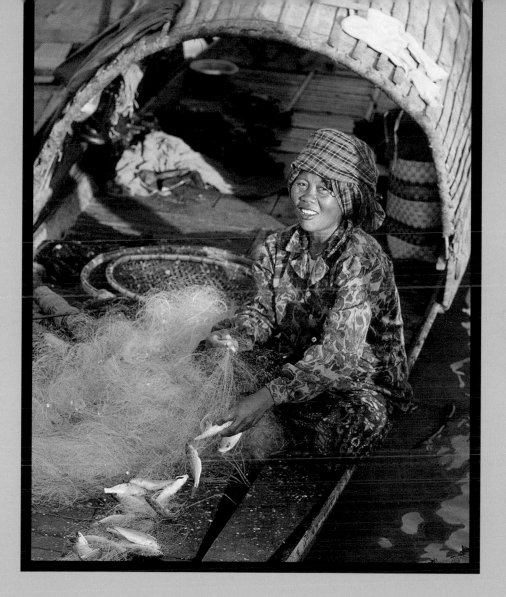

Cambodia does not have large factories and industry. Many people work in small shops repairing and making things. Fishing is important too.

Transport

Most Cambodians are too poor to buy cars. Instead people use bicycles, motorcycles and special bicycle taxis.

For long journeys Cambodians take the
bus, or go by boat. People travel by
boat on the big rivers and on the huge
Tonlé Sap lake.

Language

Cambodians speak a language called Khmer. Khmer writing goes from left to right, but there are no gaps between the words. Khmer has its own alphabet.

Khmer is very different from English. There are 100 different words for rice. There are two words for yes, one used by women, and one used by men.

School

At school Cambodian children learn to
read and write Khmer. They also learn
English. The teacher is a very important
person. The children take care to be good.

Not all young people can go to school.
There has been war in Cambodia for
more than 20 years. Lots of schools
have been destroyed. Many teachers
have been killed.

Free time

Cambodians love **festivals**. The whole family can put on their best clothes and visit their local **temple**.

Lots of Cambodian children help their parents in their free time. They help grow rice, or sell sweets and fruit to make money.

Celebrations

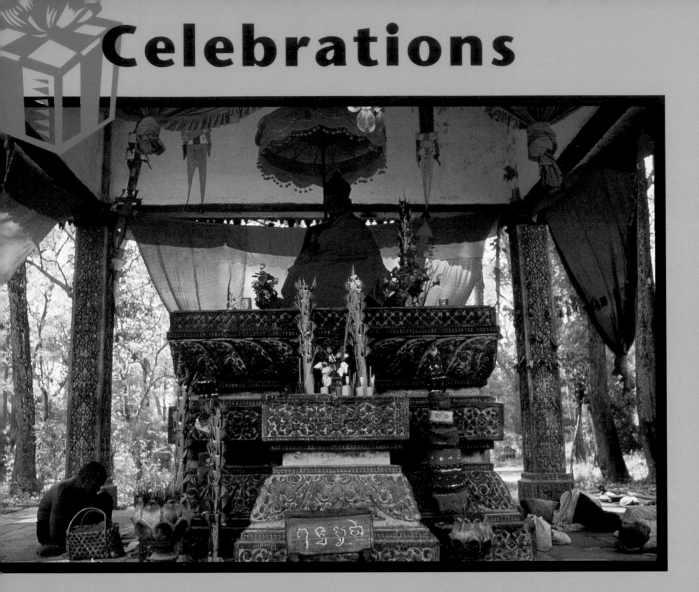

Cambodians celebrate the Khmer New Year in April. People give each other presents of new clothes, and take gifts to their local **temple**.

In the **monsoon** rains the big Tonlé Sap
River gets so full, it flows backwards.
When this happens, Cambodians have
the Water **Festival**.

The Arts

Royal dance is a very old Cambodian art. Dancers wear beautiful costumes. The dances tell stories of love and battles.

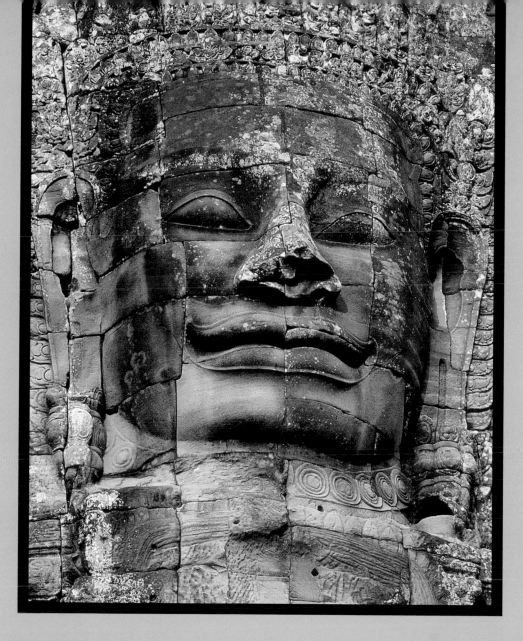

In Cambodia there are many old
carvings. Today artists still carve. They
make beautiful images of the **Buddha**.

Factfile

Name   The Kingdom of Cambodia.

Capital   Cambodia's **capital** city is called Phnom Penh.

Language   Most Cambodians speak Khmer.

Population   There are 9.5 million people living in Cambodia.

Money   Cambodians use money called reil.

Religion   Most Cambodians are **Buddhists**.

Products   Cambodia produces rice, fish, rubber, paper and wood.

Words you can learn

joom reab suor (JEWM RE-a SUE-o)   hello

bat (BAH)   yes (said by men)

jas (JAHS)   yes (said by women)

te   no

ar kun (R KUN)   thank you

suom (SUE-um)   please

pee   two

bram   five

bram-pee   seven

Glossary

Buddhist   Buddhism is a religion. Buddhists believe that if they live a good life, then they will be rewarded

Buddha   was a man who lived long ago. Buddhists follow his teachings

buffalo   a large animal that looks a bit like a cow. Buffalos are often used in Asia instead of tractors

capital   a capital city is a country's most important city. It is where the government lives

carvings   pictures made in stone or wood

chopsticks   a pair of sticks held in one hand, used to lift food to the mouth

crops   plants, such as rice, that are grown for food

festivals   are like parties, but a whole town or country joins in

monk   young men, and sometimes women, who spend time learning about a religion like Buddhism

monsoon   a name for a season with lots of rain

palm tree   a tree that has a long thin trunk, with a tuft of leaves right at the top

plough   this is the name for the job of breaking up the soil before seeds are planted

stilts   supports, like legs

temple   a special place for **Buddhists**, like a church or mosque

Index